by:

TIMBERLIN JIGGETTS

Farm animals and the sounds they make

C is for Cow,
the cow says moo.

H IS FOR HORSE,
the horse says neigh.

G is for goat,
the goat says maa.

P IS FOR PIG,
the Pig says oink.

H is for Hen,
the hen says cluck.

R is for Rooster,
the rooster says
cock-a-doodle-doo.

D is for dog,
the dog says bark.

D is for duck,
the duck says quack.

R is for rabbit,
the rabbit mutters.

B is for bull,
the bull bellows.

S is for sheep,
the sleep says baa.

D is for donkey,
the donkey says hee-haw.

C is for chick,
a baby chick says peep.

T is for turkey,
the turkey says gobble.

L is for llama, the llama hums.

the end

www.ingramcontent.com/pod-product-compliance
Ingram Content Group UK Ltd.
Pitfield, Milton Keynes, MK11 3LW, UK
UKHW021835270726
14058UKWH00001B/158